THE SPACE CHILD'S MOTHER GOOSE

THE
SPACE CHILD'S
MOTHER
GOOSE

Verses by Frederick Winsor
Illustrations by Marian Parry

A Fireside Book Published by

SIMON AND SCHUSTER   NEW YORK

A number of these poems and drawings
appeared originally in *The Atlantic*.

ORIGINALLY PUBLISHED IN 1958

ISBN 0–671–21316–4

LIBRARY OF CONGRESS CATALOG CARD NUMBER: 58–7574

MANUFACTURED IN THE UNITED STATES OF AMERICA

PRINTED BY COLORGRAPHIC OFFSET COMPANY

7   8   9   10   11   12   13   14   15

Laura, Theresa, Elizabeth, Anne,
We've covered these pages as best we can
With intricate pictures and elegant rhymes,
All suited, we trust, to your quicksilver times;
But if it's *vieux jeu* and it leaves you cold,
Forgive us, darlings, We're Awfully Old.

FOR

LAURA MARINA FELD

THERESA GORDON BEYER

ANNE DELANO STUBBS

ELIZABETH WINSOR STUBBS

THE AUTHOR AND ILLUSTRATOR acknowledge with gratitude the help and encouragement of the following:

DAVID MCCORD

EDWARD WEEKS

FERRIS GREENSLET

RENÉ BOURQUIN, our French expert

ALOIS GROH, our German expert

ADAM PARRY, our Greek expert

GRACE and ALFRED HARRIS, our Swahili experts

CHIANG YEE, our Chinese expert, who is also responsible for the beautiful calligraphy of the Chinese hen

THE SPACE CHILD'S MOTHER GOOSE

1

Probable-Possible, my black hen,
She lays eggs in the Relative When.
She doesn't lay eggs in the Positive Now
Because she's unable to Postulate How.

2

Little Miss Muffet
Sits on her tuffet
In a nonchalant sort of a way.
With her force field around her
The spider, the bounder,
Is not in the picture today.

A Follower of Goddard
  And a rising Astrogator
Were agreed that superthermics
  Was a spatial hot pertater.

They reached a Super-Nova
  On a bicycle named Beta
And I'd tell you more about it
  But they fused with all the data.

There was a man in our town,
4　An Astrophysicist,
　　Who found a place
　　In Hyperspace
By just a twist of wrist.

But when he sought the Nearer Now
And gave another twist,
　　He found that he'd
　　Become somehow
A Cyberneticist.

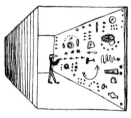

 HYPERSPACE:　Regular space is high and wide;
　　　　　　　　　Hyperspace is just outside.

5

Little Bo-Peep
Has lost her sheep,
The radar has failed to find them.
They'll all, face to face,
Meet in parallel space,
Preceding their leaders behind them.

BC
AD

1500

1900

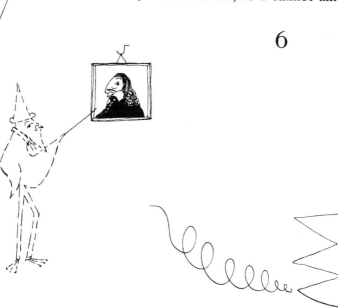

There was an old man in a Time Machine
Who borrowed a Tuesday all painted green.
His pockets with rockets he used to jam
And he said, "I have thunk, so I cannot am!"

6

7   This is the way the Physicist rides:
A quantum, a quantum, a quantum.

This is the way the Agronomist rides:
I plant 'em, I plant 'em, I plant 'em.

This is the way the Philosopher rides:
O Plato!   O Plato!   O Plato!

This is the way the Rocketman rides:
JATO!   JATO!!   JATO!!!

QUANTUM: The *Quantum* is only a tittle or jot:
On a little theory hangs a lot.

8 Three jolly sailors from Blaydon-on-Tyne
They went to sea in a bottle by Klein.
Since the sea was entirely inside the hull
The scenery seen was exceedingly dull.

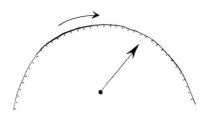

The Jack Spratt
Commissariat
Included the fat and the lean,
But a Chronoloid move
Was found to improve
The Continuum in the cuisine.

9,

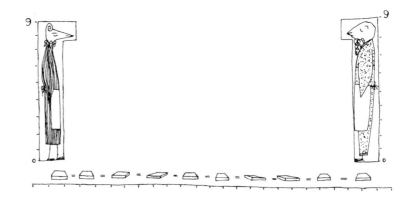

Plus-que-Possible, ma poule noire,
Elle pond ses oeufs dans le Quand-Provisoire.
Elle ne pond point dans une période sure
Car l'expérience serait bien trop dure.

10

This little pig built a spaceship,
   This little pig paid the bill;
This little pig made isotopes,
   This little pig ate a pill;
And this little pig did nothing at all,
   But he's just a little pig still.

11

There was an old woman with notions quite new,
She never told children the things they should do.
She hoisted the covers up over her head
When people explained where her theories led.

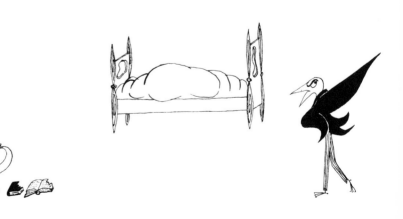

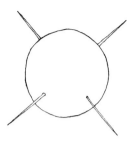

 12

Spin along in spatial night,
Artificial Satellite;
Monitor, with blip and beep,
The Universe—and Baby's sleep.

BLIP *and* BLEEP: Twixt Radar's *Blip*
             And *Beep* of Telephone
        The well-screened man
            Can't call his soul his own.

13   A Space Child would exploring go.
        Heigh! Ho! says Rowley.
     A Space Child would exploring go
     Whether his mother would let him or no,
  With a rowley, powley, gammon and spinach,
      Heigh Ho! says Anthony Rowley.

     He traveled in space till he reached the brink.
       Heigh! Ho! says Rowley.
     He traveled in space till he reached the brink
     And developed a thirst for galacteal drink,
  With a sipper, a supper, a tankard of copper,
      Heigh Ho! says Anthony Rowley.

The cube of a spiral equation uncurled.
Heigh! Ho! says Rowley.
The cube of a spiral equation uncurled
And he reached a rather improbable world,
With a raggle, a taggle, ten geese in a gaggle,
Heigh Ho! says Anthony Rowley.

He traveled at quite an impossible rate.
Heigh! Ho! says Rowley.
He traveled at quite an impossible rate
For his mind could prestidigitate,
With a snippet, a tippet, a lop and a lippet,
Heigh Ho! says Anthony Rowley.

He argued with Atropos' sister crones.
   Heigh! Ho! says Rowley.
He argued with Atropos' sister crones
In supersonical overtones,
With a chattering, nattering patter of clatter,
   Heigh Ho! says Anthony Rowley.

He traveled till Near was further than Far.
   Heigh! Ho! says Rowley.
He traveled till Near was further than Far
And covered the course in well under par,
With a kickin', a flickin', to quicken the chicken,
   Heigh Ho! says Anthony Rowley.

He traveled in Time till a trick in the track.
　Heigh! Ho! says Rowley.
He traveled in Time till a trick in the track
Uncovered his own retreating back,
With a skirting exerting a force for reverting,
　Heigh Ho! says Anthony Rowley.

His mother undressed him and put him to bed.
　Heigh! Ho! says Rowley.
His mother undressed him and put him to bed
And affixed the Deep-Freeze to the top of his head,
With a thrilling, a chilling, a feeling unwilling,
　Heigh Ho! says Anthony Rowley.

14

Flappity, Floppity, Flip!
The Mouse on the Möbius Strip.
  The Strip revolved,
  The Mouse dissolved
In a chronodimensional skip.

15

"Pussy cat, pussy cat,
    What do you see
That enlarges your tail
    To this noble degree?"

"I see a small
    Four-dimensional man
Who has recently landed
    From Aldebaran."

"Pussy cat, pussy cat,
    What do you hear
To cause that irrational
    Twitch of your ear?"

"I hear the lullaby
    Mother cats croon
To the play-weary kittens
    On Jupiter's moon."

16   Said the Cortex
      To the Vortex
   "Won't you have a Chlorophyll?"
      Said the Vortex
      To the Cortex
   "Thank you, sir, perhaps I will."

CORTEX: The *Cortex* wraps around a core.
          Alas! There isn't any vore.

17

Little Jack Horner
Sits in a corner
Extracting cube roots to infinity,
An assignment for boys
That will minimize noise
And produce a more peaceful vicinity.

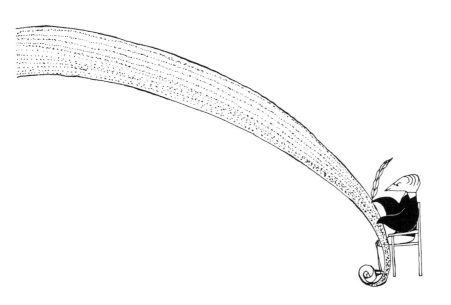

18.

Gay go forth, and gay go far,
To know the song of every star.

❊ ❊ ❊

"Obey the Space Laws, rash young man,"
Enjoins the great Aldebaran.

"Never scorn a chart to use,"
Says the careful Betelgeuse.

"With traffic thick, beware the fool,"
Postulates Algol, the Ghoul.

"Even Hyperspace is narrow,"
Says Arcturus, of the Arrow.

"Watch the heavy-water seal,"
Says Canopus, at the Wheel.

"Miscalculation's fuel's drain,"
Thus says Spica, Ear of Grain.

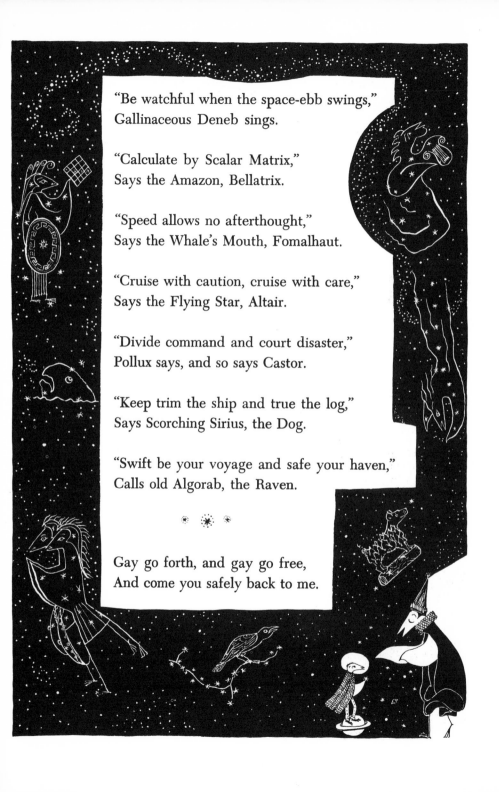

"Be watchful when the space-ebb swings,"
Gallinaceous Deneb sings.

"Calculate by Scalar Matrix,"
Says the Amazon, Bellatrix.

"Speed allows no afterthought,"
Says the Whale's Mouth, Fomalhaut.

"Cruise with caution, cruise with care,"
Says the Flying Star, Altair.

"Divide command and court disaster,"
Pollux says, and so says Castor.

"Keep trim the ship and true the log,"
Says Scorching Sirius, the Dog.

"Swift be your voyage and safe your haven,"
Calls old Algorab, the Raven.

✷ ❋ ✷

Gay go forth, and gay go free,
And come you safely back to me.

Möglich-Warscheinlich, mein' Schwartzhenn',
Legt ihr Ei in das Relativwenn.
Sie legt keine Eier ins Positivdann
Weil sie postulieren nun einmal nicht kann.

19.

See the little phrases go,
   Watch their funny antics.
The men who make them wiggle so
   Are teachers of Semantics.

The words go up, the words go round
   And make a great commotion,
But all that lies behind the sound
   Is hebetude Bœotian.

20

Russell and Whitehead and Hegel and Kant!
Maybe I shall and maybe I shan't.

Maybe I shan't and maybe I shall.
Kant Russell Whitehead, Hegel et al.

21

Peter Pater
Astrogator
Lost his orbit calculator
Out among the asteroids . . .

They rang the Lutine Bell at Lloyd's.

'Αλεκτρυὼν φίλη 'στί μοι, τῇ οὔνομ' ἐστιν Εἰκός·
τὰ δ' ῷὰ τίκτει τῷ λόγῳ, σοφίστρι' ὄρνις οὖσα·
ἔργῳ μὲν οὔ· τί γὰρ πλέον; κρείσσων λόγος γὰρ ἔργου.

I have a pet hen whose name is Probable. She lays eggs in
concept, being a sophist-bird. But not in reality at all; those
would be inferior eggs; for thought is superior to reality.

22

Solomon Grundy
Walked on Monday
Rode on Tuesday
Motored Wednesday
Planed on Thursday
Rocketed Friday
Spaceship Saturday
Time Machine Sunday
Where is the end for
Solomon Grundy?

23   Hey Diddle Diddle
Distribute the Middle
The Premise controls the Conclusion
The Disjunctive affirms
That the Diet of Worms
Is a Borbetomagic confusion.

24

If holidays were twelve months long
And Life were games and fun
  And all the skies
  Were filled with PSI's
Would Thinking still get done?

25

Resistor, transistor, condensers in pairs,
Battery, platter, record me some airs;
Squeaker and squawker and woofer times pi,
And Baby shall have his own private Hi-Fi.

WOOFER: The *Woofer,* as its name implies,
Will sound the lows but not the highs.

Taffy was a Welshman,
   Taffy was a thief.
Taffy's little grandson
   Teleplunders beef.

Taffy's little grandson
   Cymric superlooter,
Looks angelic riding
   His teledriven scooter.

Taffy's little grandson
   Never leaves the village,
Stays at home in comfort
   Committing telepillage.

Taffy's little grandson,
   Practicing psionics,
Quite surpasses Grandpa's
   Obsolete kleptonics.

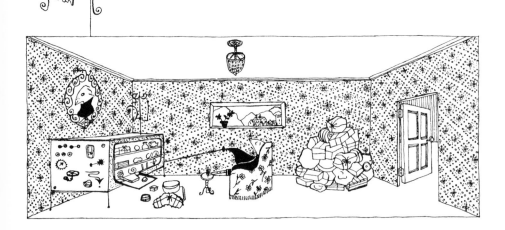

CYMRIC: The *Cymric* bard is one whose wails
Originate—surprise!—in Wales.

TELEPLUNDER, TELEPILLAGE, *etc.*: The mind can weave a wonderful spell,
It has no need of Graham Bell.
It used to keep its secrets well,
But now, when you kiss, it'll *Tele*tell.

PSIONICS: *Psionics: there's* a potent think:
The Mind sets mountains totterink.

KLEPTONICS: Pillage, petit larceny and spoliation;
Prigging, plunder, piracy and depredation;
Pocket-picking, pilfering and peculation:
Kleptonic all, and Ethic Divagation.

27   Venus Vermiculate,
    Be my own BEM.
How bright is that eye
    On its seven-foot stem.

Croon in that sweet
    Ophicleidean voice
And we two shall in true
    Symbiosis rejoice.

BEM: A Bug-Eyed Monster, that's the *BEM,*
       E.g. The child—ad hominem.

SYMBIOSIS: The Panting Lover says—I quote—
       "Darling, you're my *Symbiote;*
       Without you, dear, I'm like to die."
       Lovers still, you'll notice, lie.

28

See Saw
Margery Daw
Recurs in a future dimension.
Since, in the past,
She won't work very fast,
Her wages are held in suspension.

29

Embryonic, zoonic,
Tectonic, cyclonic,
We humans are never humane.
Explosion, erosion,
Corrosion, implosion—
And back into Chaos again!

Matago ya kuku mweusi, nadhani,
Ni mbali, mbele au nyuma;
Haikuta mayai kuku huku au sasa—
Ni kwa hivi haipatikani.

I suspect that the egg-laying locales of the black hen
Are far away in-front-or-behind in-either-time-or-space;
She doesn't lay eggs here on this very spot or now—
Because of this eggs are not obtainable.

30

This is the Theory Jack built.

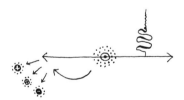

This is the Flaw
That lay in the Theory Jack built.

This is the Mummery
Hiding the Flaw
That lay in the Theory Jack built.

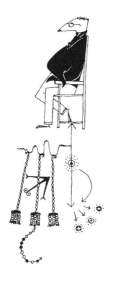

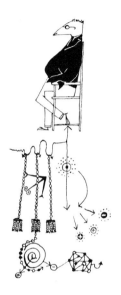

This is the Summary
Based on the Mummery
Hiding the Flaw
That lay in the Theory Jack built.

This is the Constant K
That saved the Summary
Based on the Mummery
Hiding the Flaw
That lay in the Theory Jack built.

This is the Erudite Verbal Haze
Cloaking Constant K
That saved the Summary
Based on the Mummery
Hiding the Flaw
That lay in the Theory Jack built.

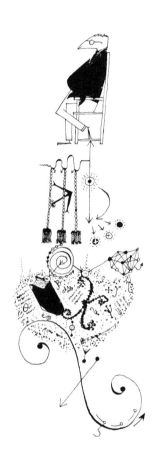

This is the Turn of a Plausible Phrase
That thickened the Erudite Verbal Ha
Cloaking Constant **K**
That saved the Summary
Based on the Mummery
Hiding the Flaw
That lay in the Theory Jack built.

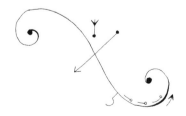

This is Chaotic Confusion and Bluff
That hung on the Turn of a Plausible Phrase
That thickened the Erudite Verbal Haze
Cloaking Constant K
That saved the Summary
Based on the Mummery
Hiding the Flaw
That lay in the Theory Jack built.

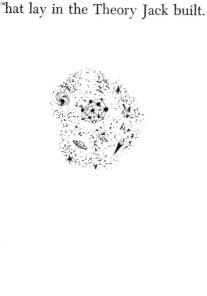

This is the Cybernetics and Stuff
That covered Chaotic Confusion and Bluff
That hung on the Turn of a Plausible Phrase
And thickened the Erudite Verbal Haze
Cloaking Constant **K**
That saved the Summary
Based on the Mummery
Hiding the Flaw
That lay in the Theory Jack built.

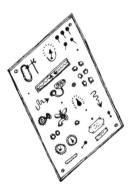

This is the Button to Start the Machine
To make with the Cybernetics and Stuff
To cover Chaotic Confusion and Bluff
That hung on the Turn of a Plausible Phrase
And thickened the Erudite Verbal Haze
Cloaking Constant **K**
That saved the Summary
Based on the Mummery
Hiding the Flaw
That lay in the Theory Jack built.

This is the Space Child with Brow Serene
Who pushed the Button to Start the Machine
That made with the Cybernetics and Stuff
Without Confusion, exposing the Bluff
That hung on the Turn of a Plausible Phrase
And, shredding the Erudite Verbal Haze
Cloaking Constant K
Wrecked the Summary
Based on the Mummery
Hiding the Flaw
And Demolished the Theory Jack built.

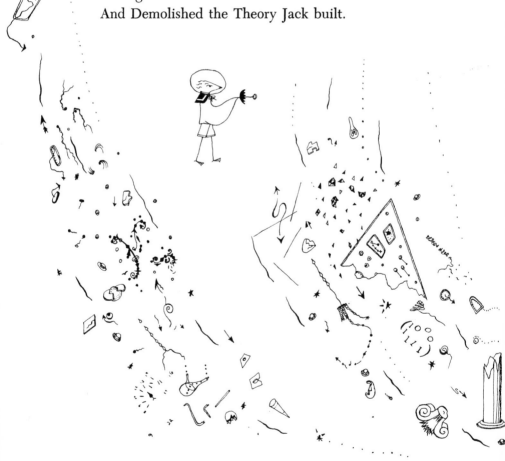

31

Titus FitzImmeter
Said, "The Planimeter
  Agoragraphs a vicinity."
Herein he was right,
But he scarcely shed light
  On the Circular Points at Infinity.

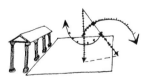

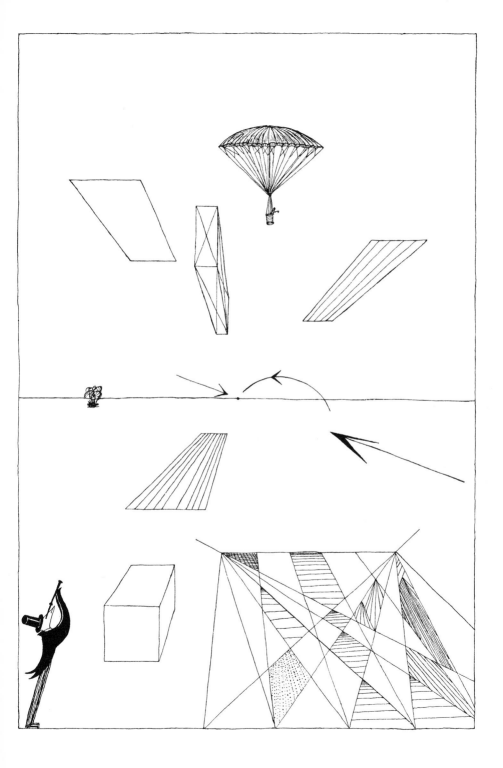

32

Automation
Is vexation,
Quaternions are bad;
Analysis Situs
Is only detritus,
I wonder: Have I been had?

෬33ᶜ

The Colloid and the Crystalloid
  Were fighting just in jest.
The Colloid called the Crystalloid
  A Pseudo-Anapest.

Some thought them physical
  And some thought them chemic—
And some said the whole affair
  Was slightly academic.

PSEUDO—ANAPEST: The *Pseudo-Anapest*
                         Moves awkwardly at best;
                         His feet are long, uneven and retractile.
                         Who hunts the beast in rhythm
                         Should take his meter withm
                         And *still* may only bag a Ptero-Dactyl.

34

One is just half of the old Snake's Eyes—
Flying saucers are filling the skies.

The Trey is followed by Little Joe—
Antigravity makes them go.

The Feever's eye is on Dixie's Six—
Sound the alarm if the space-drive sticks.

Seven from Heaven and Eight from Decatur—
Hope for the best from the Astrogator.

Nona Peptona pursues Big Ten—
Rockets blast as the Captain says "When!"

Eleven, and then, with a pair of Box Cars,
The spaceship is wrecked on the Desert of Mars.

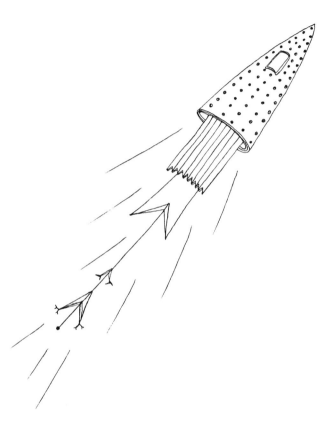

 NONA PEPTONA: *Nona Peptona* and similar names
Are derived from ritual counting games.

35

The Hydrogen Dog and the Cobalt Cat
Side by side in the Armory sat.
Nobody thought about fusion or fission,
Everyone spoke of their peacetime mission,
    Till somebody came and opened the door.
There they were, in a neutron fog,
The Codrogen Cat and the Hybalt Dog;
    They mushroomed up with a terrible roar—
    And Nobody Never was there—Nomore.

36

Geniac, Geniac,
   Digital miracle,
Giving an answer that's
   Truly empirical.
Learned men, lost in a
   Drawjopping daze,
Watch six-year-old Seniors, all
   Grabbing off A's.

37

Rock and Roll
With self-control,
My Cybernetic Baby;
The Laws of Mede
And Persian need
That infants heed them—maybe.

Foundations shake,
Computers break
And Science goes Be-bop,
But Baby's joy
Is still the toy
With foolish ears that flop.

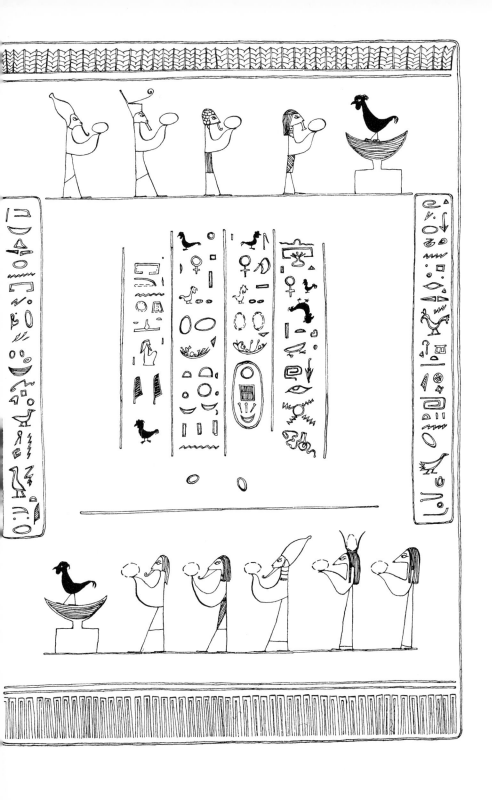

"Mary, Mary,
    Quite contrary,
How are your Hydroponics?"
    "I've Dixie Belles
    And chanterelles
All singing in Supersonics."

38

 HYDROPONICS: I watch things grow,
       And O, my heart gives thanks
You need not hoe
    In *Hydroponic* tanks.

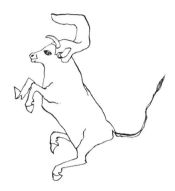

39

Little Boy Blue
   Call the Space Patrol,
The cows are dancing
   The Carmagnole.

The sheep have mutated
   To sable-furred cod
And even the pigs are
   Quadratic'lly odd.

MUTANTS: Had *Mutants* never changed the pace
             Would Man yet lead the Reptile Race?

40

Hark, hark,
A static spark,
The tape is wound around
So some baboon
Can croon his tune
In Stereophonic Sound.

41

Humpty Dumpty sat on a wall.
At three o'clock he had his great fall.
The King set the Time Machine back to two.
Now Humpty's unscrambled and good as new.

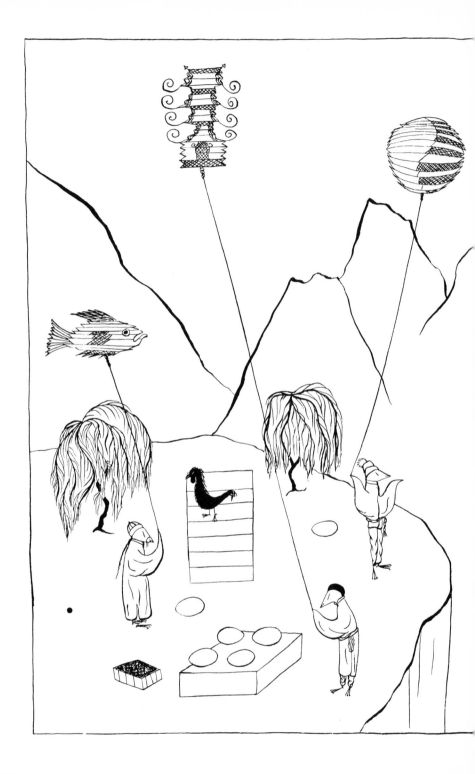

庶幾可兮黑母雞
伊生蛋兮有其期
而今確定不生蛋
祇為無從告隱私

It is likely possible the Black Hen
She has definite periods to lay eggs.
Now it is certain that she will not lay any egg
For her secret cannot be disclosed.

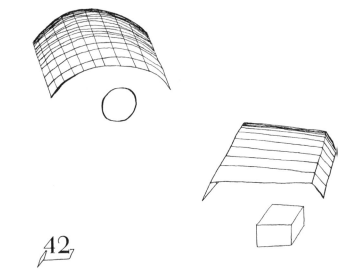

42

Orientable planes,
Their stresses and strains—
And my story is well on its way;
An erudite thesis
On Psychokinesis—
And that will be all for today.

43

The Pimlico Dream
 Of the Bloomsbury Group
May have made Mayfair
 A Keynesington Soup.

44

Data scrutator,
Extrapolator,
You forecast by rigadoon.
You used to extol
The Gallup Poll
But now you are shooting the moon.

45   Sing a song of saucers
         Flown from outer space.
      Four-and-twenty generals,
         Crimson in the face.

      The saucers conquered gravity
         So they all began to spin—
      And, Gentlemen, if you'll pardon me,
         This is where I came in.

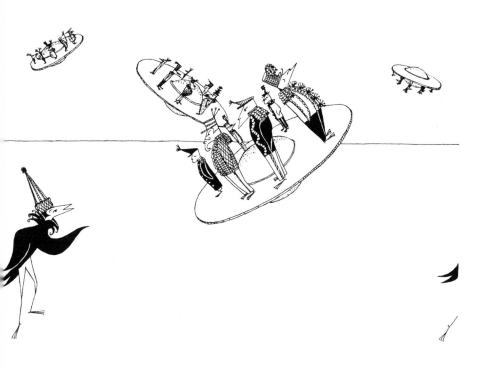

THE ANSWERS

agoragraph. To measure the area of an enclosed plane surface by tracing the boundary with a planimeter.

agronomist. Agricultural specialist in the theory and practice of field crop production and soil management; a farmer with a Ph.D.

analysis situs. Mathematical study of properties of a geometrical configuration unchanged when the configuration is subjected to any one-to-one continuous transformation; rubber-sheet geometry.

astrogator. Officer in charge of plotting course and directing spaceship beyond the atmospheric limits of the earth.

Atropos. That one of the three Fates who cut the thread for Clotho and Lachesis.

BEM. Bug-Eyed Monster; any fearsome non-humanoid creature from outer space, or from beyond our ken (*Coll.*, S-F).

Bloomsbury Group. 20th-century artistic and literary group with a tendency toward classicism in the arts if not in economics; mostly resident about Bloomsbury.

Bœotian. Person of Bœotia, reputedly the dullest part of ancient Greece; hence the superlative in stupidity.

Borbetomagic. Pertaining to the ancient city of Borbetomagus, now Worms; the transition of names is obscure.

chanterelle. Weakness, sore point (Fr. *appuyer sur la chanterelle*); edible mushroom.

CHANTERELLE.

chronoloid. Concept, real or imaginary, having the appearance but not the reality of Time; analogous to the *horizontal promotion.*

colloid. Formerly regarded as a special type of matter; now considered to be matter in, or apparently in, a particular state of subdivision, and subject to *Brownian movement.*

continuum. Perfect connected aggregate of n dimensions when each element corresponds to a set of simultaneous values of n independent real variables $x_1 \ldots x_n$; analogous to a piece of string or the debates of the United States Senate.

crystalloid. (cf. *colloid*) Crystalloids are separated from colloids by dialysis, or filtering through a membrane, and usually crystallize under suitable conditions.

cybernetics. Comparative study of the control systems of humans and computing machines; loosely *the mathematics of human behavior;* its invention and development is generally attributed to *Professor Norbert Wiener.*

cyclonic. Of the nature of a rotary storm; sudden and devastating.

Cymric. Brythonic.

disjunctive. Proposition expressing alternatives.

Dixie Belle. Southern beauty: applied to silver mines, steamboats, stimulants, etc.

extrapolating. Calculating the unknown outside from the known inside; interpolating backwards.

force field. Region covered by force of unspecified origin and immense power, usually a defense mechanism (S-F).

galacteal. Having to do with a galaxy, *fig.* with the Milky Way.

gallinaceous. Pertaining to the Galliformes; a fowl word.

GALLIFORMES.

Geniac. Trade name of a do-it-yourself thinking machine.

Goddard, Robert H. The father of rocketry.

heavy-water seal. Deuterium oxide used as protection or cooling element for space-drive mechanism.

hebetude. Dullness.

hyperspace. Space of more than three dimensions; neat for galacteal travelers.

implosion. Busting in instead of out.

isotope. One of two or more elements with the same atomic number which are distinguished by radioactive transformations.

JATO. Jet-assisted take-off.

Keynes, J. M. Economist; member of the Bloomsbury Group.

J. M. KEYNES.

Klein bottle. Container whose inner and outer surfaces are one; cf. *Möbius strip* and *orientable.*

kleptonics. Art or science of theft.

Lutine bell. Bell rung at Lloyd's when a vessel is reported missing; also rung when a missing vessel is sighted.

Möbius strip. Strip formed into a ring with a half-twist, thereby producing an object with only one side

MOBIUS STRIP.

and one edge; also known as *M. sheet* or *M. ring.*

mutate. To vary suddenly (*biol.*).

neutron. Uncharged particle in an atomic nucleus, of nearly the mass of the proton; an impartial particle.

ophicleide. Wooden serpent with keys added; predecessor of the Sousaphone.

OPHICLEIDE.

orientable. A two-dimensional manifold is orientable when no portion thereof is homeomorphic with a Möbius strip, q.v.

parallel space. Loosely, a space continuum existing entirely outside another space continuum.

planimeter. Instrument for the agoragraphy of an enclosed plane surface by tracing its boundary.

pseudo-anapest. False or defective anapest.

PSI. General and S-F term for hypermental powers.

psionics. Usually, the control of machines by the mind.

psychokinesis. Application of physical force by mental power; ineffectively practiced by harassed parents.

quantum. Elemental unit of energy; quantum mechanics are said to have made possible nuclear physics.

quaternion. Operator or factor, multiplication by which converts a vector into another vector.

QUATERNIONS.

resistor. Device for control, protection or operation of electric circuit through electrical resistance.

rigadoon. Lively jumping dance; music, therefore, usually in duple or triple time.

scalar matrix. Square matrix with each element zero except those on the principal diagonal, and which has each of its elements equal to the same number.

semantics. The science of meanings; considered by some to be a deliberate confusion.

space-ebb. Hypothetical flowing out of space; S-F does not disclose what remains after space has run out.

squawker. Loud speaker.

squeaker. High speaker.

stereophonic. Sounding in both ears; analogous to babies.

Super-Nova. Very large star, suddenly increasing in light and energy.

supersonics. Science of sound too high to be heard.

superthermics. Science of heat too hot to be felt.

symbiotes. Dissimilar organisms living in more or less intimate association; only faintly analogous to domestic bliss.

tectonic. Indicating forces resulting from deformation of the earth's crust.

vermiculate. Sophistical; wormlike.

woofer. Low speaker.

zoonic. Pertaining to animals. ANIMAL.